LIV

SYRIA

ABDO
Publishing Company

SYRIA

Dale Evva Gelfand

Content Consultant
Elizabeth Shakman Hurd
Associate Professor, Political Science, Northwestern University

CREDITS

Published by ABDO Publishing Company, PO Box 398166, Minneapolis, MN 55439.
Copyright © 2013 by Abdo Consulting Group, Inc. International copyrights reserved
in all countries. No part of this book may be reproduced in any form without written
permission from the publisher. The Essential Library™ is a trademark and logo of
ABDO Publishing Company.

Printed in the United States of America,
North Mankato, Minnesota
112012
012013

 THIS BOOK CONTAINS AT LEAST 10% RECYCLED MATERIALS.

Editor: Arnold Ringstad
Series Designer: Emily Love

About the Author: Having taught herself to read at the tender age of three, Dale Evva
Gelfand was destined to be a wordsmith—and for some 30 years she has happily plied
her craft as writer and editor. When not reading, she can be found tending her gardens,
hiking the woods with her beloved mutt, and photographing the world around the
upstate New York home that she shares with her likewise beloved significant other.

Cataloging-in-Publication Data

Gelfand, Dale Evva.
 Syria / Dale Evva Gelfand.
   p. cm. -- (Countries of the world)
Includes bibliographical references and index.
ISBN 978-1-61783-639-8
1. Syria--Juvenile literature.   I. Title.
956.91--dc22

2012946084

Cover: A Syrian castle

TABLE OF CONTENTS

CHAPTER 1
A VISIT TO SYRIA

Your Syrian adventure begins when your airplane lands in the northern city of Aleppo. Located near the Turkish border, Aleppo boasts 8,000 years of history and is one of the oldest continuously inhabited cities on earth. Aleppo is the country's most populated city and the commercial center of Syria. The dynamic energy of Aleppo has captivated travelers for centuries, and the promise of an unforgettable experience strikes you the moment your taxi enters the city in a whir of traffic.

Finally, you exit the taxi and get your bearings. As you orient yourself toward the Old City, you note that many of the people you see are young and wearing Western-style dress: men in shirtsleeves and long pants, women in modest blouses and pants or skirts. Many urban women in Syria readily adopted Western clothing following World War I (1914–1918). However, this is not

Aleppo has a population of more than 2 million people.

Aleppo is a busy, modern city with thousands of years of history.

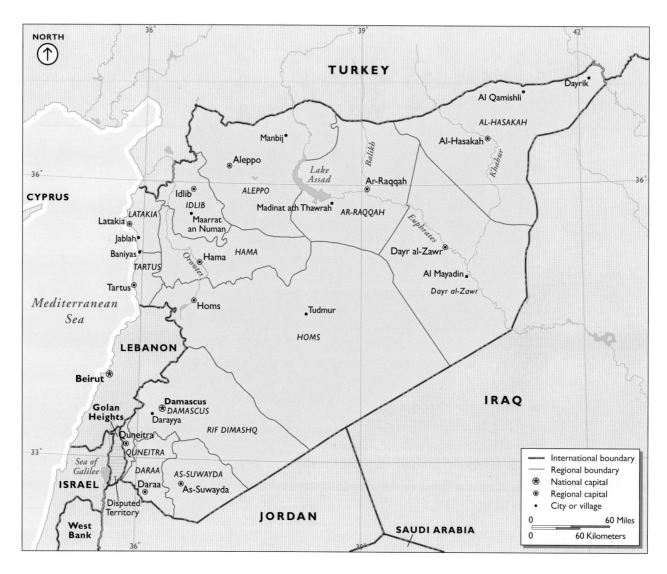

NORTH
↑

TURKEY

Dayrik

Al Qamishli

AL-HASAKAH

Manbij

Al-Hasakah

Aleppo

Lake Assad

Balikh

Khabur

CYPRUS

Idlib

ALEPPO

Ar-Raqqah

Madinat ath Thawrah

AR-RAQQAH

Euphrates

LATAKIA

Latakia

Maarrat an Numan

Dayr al-Zawr

Jablah

Orontes

Baniyas

HAMA

Hama

Al Mayadin

TARTUS

Dayr al-Zawr

Tartus

Mediterranean Sea

Homs

Tudmur

HOMS

LEBANON

Beirut

IRAQ

Damascus
DAMASCUS

Golan Heights

Darayya

Quneitra

RIF DIMASHQ

QUNEITRA

Sea of Galilee

DARAA

AS-SUWAYDA

ISRAEL

Daraa

As-Suwayda

Disputed Territory

JORDAN

SAUDI ARABIA

West Bank

———	International boundary
———	Regional boundary
⊛	National capital
◉	Regional capital
•	City or village

0   60 Miles

0   60 Kilometers

Political Boundaries of Syria

the case in rural areas, where more conservative traditional clothing is typical.

The division between old and new Aleppo is striking. The Old City is enclosed within a seven-gated wall built in medieval times. If not for the passersby in modern clothing, you might well be standing in the twelfth century—the architecture has remained largely unchanged since then. The United Nations Educational, Scientific and Cultural Organization (UNESCO) has declared the Old City a World Heritage Site, and it is easy to see why. You feel the sheer age of the place as you wander its maze of narrow cobblestone lanes, admiring the intricately decorated facades of the buildings.

You are on your way to the medieval castle known as the Citadel, the focal point of Aleppo. The fabled fortress has loomed over the city

THE FORGOTTEN CITIES

Scattered across the limestone hills to the north and west of Aleppo are the architectural remains of nearly 800 abandoned villages dating from between the first and seventh centuries.[1] Known collectively as the Forgotten Cities, these ruins lay largely forgotten and undisturbed for more than a millennium. They exemplify the transition from the Roman Empire to the Byzantine Empire and give an unprecedented glimpse into rural life in that era. Though abandoned by the tenth century, many of the stone structures are in an amazing state of preservation. Among the structures are private homes, pagan temples, monasteries, inns, Christian churches, markets, and bathhouses, all still connected by paved streets.

since the twelfth century. Constructed on a fortified outcropping rising above the city, and accessible by a vast arched bridge, the Citadel was originally built to guard and protect the surrounding agricultural areas. The entire structure measures 1,476 feet (450 m) long by 1,066 feet (325 m) wide.[2]

ANCIENT CIVILIZATION, NEW COUNTRY

Syria has seen empires come and go, leaving behind deep cultural legacies. It has embraced a diversity of ethnicities and religions, folding them into the rich tapestry that makes up this nation. But its actual nationhood is quite young. And until the twentieth century, the name Syria referred not to the defined boundaries known today but to Greater Syria, which included all of modern Syria as well as Lebanon, Palestine, Jordan, and parts of southern Turkey.

After thousands of years of conquest and occupation, Syria was recognized as an independent state in April 1946. Ancient Syria was a land shaped by a vast array of civilizations. Contemporary Syria is still struggling to find its identity in the twenty-first century.

You walk a few streets over to admire the Great Mosque, with its striking eleventh-century square minaret. Families often picnic at its black and white stone-patterned courtyard. Directly opposite the mosque stands the twelfth-century Madrasa Halawiye, which was once the sixth-century Cathedral of Saint Helena. You are reminded that for centuries, Syrian Christians acted as intermediaries with the European merchants who came to trade for Aleppo's goods.

The Great Mosque in Aleppo is the city's largest and oldest mosque.

THE WONDERS OF THE SOUQ

After you have taken in some of the ancient marvels of the Old City, you decide to head for the souq, or marketplace. Given that trade has always been a part of Aleppo, it is no surprise that Aleppo's souqs are deemed the best in Syria. These living museums date as far back as the thirteenth century, when goods from China and central Asia mingled with those from the eastern Mediterranean. Aleppo's largest souq includes some seven miles (12 km) of covered markets, comprising the longest covered souq in the Middle East.[3] It winds through labyrinthine lanes and alleyways, linking mosques, madrasas, bathhouses, and inns.

You navigate the teeming narrow lanes with their soaring vaulted-brick ceilings and hundreds of stalls, seemingly going back and forth in time as you dodge carts hauled by donkeys and speeding motorbikes. You savor the sights and smells of

THE SOUQS

Centuries ago, the souqs became known by the products they sold. The Souq Al-Attareen sold perfume, the Souq Al-Saagha sold jewelry, the Souq Khan Al-Nahaseen sold copper goods, and the Souq Al-Haddadeen sold iron goods. Perhaps most famous of all is the Souq Al-Saboun, the Soap Souq. Here Aleppo's specialty, a laurel-leaf and olive-oil soap, has been sold for hundreds of years and is still available today.

Inside a souq, vendors sell items ranging from jewelry to clothes to food.

In 2012, the US Department of State advised all US citizens to avoid visiting Syria. A crisis between insurgents and government military forces had already resulted in thousands of dead and wounded citizens. The State Department counseled travelers that because of the Syrian government's intense scrutiny of citizens and foreigners alike, any interaction with a local by a visitor might result in an investigation by Syrian officials, especially if the interaction is considered political in nature. Those choosing to visit Syria despite this warning were advised to steer clear of any public protests and political gatherings, to avoid suspicious behavior, and to always carry proof of identity.

Syria's poor relations with Israel resulted in a further warning for travelers. Anyone holding a passport bearing Israeli visas or even entry/exit stamps indicating travel to Israel was banned from entering Syria. Likewise, if a traveler had visited a country adjacent to Israel but their passport lacked entry stamps from that country, Syrian immigration officials would refuse admittance. US citizens suspected of having traveled to Israel have been detained for questioning by Syrian authorities.

handwoven fabrics, clothes, jewelry, spices, perfume, and pastries. Colorful, intricately woven carpets hang all around you.

The labyrinth eventually leads you to an exit, and you're back across from the Citadel, by a sidewalk café. Deciding it is the perfect spot to enjoy a Syrian coffee, you sit, recoup your energy, and admire your newfound treasures.

TROUBLE IN SYRIA

While the rich history and culture of Syria are enticing, events in 2011 and 2012 made it a dangerous

Widespread street protests began in Syria in March 2011.

place to visit. An uprising against the autocratic president of Syria was launched in March 2011, and the government's violent crackdowns resulted in the deaths of many Syrians.

The nation faced many challenges in the early twenty-first century, with this political upheaval being the most prominent. However, it was not the only problem faced by Syrians. Economic troubles, compounded by political circumstances, made everyday life more challenging for the nation's citizens. At the same time, environmental degradation threatened many of the plants and animals that were the region's original inhabitants. With these challenges ahead of them, Syrians seeking reforms and change counted on the passion and energy of their young people to steer the country toward brighter days ahead.

The United Nations began calling the conflict in Syria a civil war in July 2012.

SNAPSHOT

Official name: Syrian Arab Republic

Capital city: Damascus

Form of government: republic (under authoritarian military-dominated Arab Socialist Ba'ath Party regimes since March 1963)

Titles of leaders: president (chief of state), prime minister (head of government)

Currency: Syrian pound

Population (July 2012 est.): 22,530,746
World rank: 53

Size: 71,498 square miles (185,180 sq km), including 500 square miles (1,295 sq km) of Israeli-occupied territory
World rank: 89

Language: Arabic (official); also Kurdish, Armenian, Aramaic, Circassian, English, and French

Official religion: none (Unofficial religion: Islam, 90 percent of population)

Per capita GDP (2011, US dollars) $5,100
World rank: 151

CHAPTER 2

GEOGRAPHY: TOPOGRAPHIC DIVERSITY

Some countries in the Middle East are identified by their geographic features. Egypt has the Nile River, Iran has mountains, and Saudi Arabia has deserts. Syria, however, does not have such an iconic geographic distinction. Instead, it possesses a wide array of landscapes. This diversity, ranging from naturally irrigated lowlands to vast desert steppes, has played a vital role in shaping the country's historical and cultural development.

Syria's location at an area where Silk Road caravans converged made it a hub for ancient trade routes. The economic activity helped those early settlements flourish into prosperous cities. At the same

Lush vegetation exists adjacent to desolate deserts within Syria's widely varied landscape.

time, the mountains and isolated steppes provided areas where minority populations could thrive without intrusion or interference.

Syria is divided into 14 administrative areas called governates. Each is divided into districts and subdistricts. The national capital, Damascus, is in the southwest of the country and comprises its own governate.

LOCATION AND LAND

Mediterranean beaches, stark limestone steppes, profuse spring wildflowers, and lush vineyards and olive groves share the country with great expanses of desert.

Syria is bounded to the north by Turkey, to the south by Jordan, to the east and southeast by Iraq, and to the southwest by Lebanon and Israel. Four general topographic regions make up Syria: the coastal plain, hills and mountains, steppe, and desert plateau. The country is also roughly divided into western and eastern zones. The western zone, a band running from Aleppo in the north to Damascus in the south, is home to most of the population. Along with the Mediterranean coastal plain, this band includes two mountain ranges running parallel to the sea and cultivated valleys along the rivers. The eastern region is largely steppe and desert, though the Euphrates River and its tributaries provide some irrigation.

Syria is approximately the size of North Dakota.

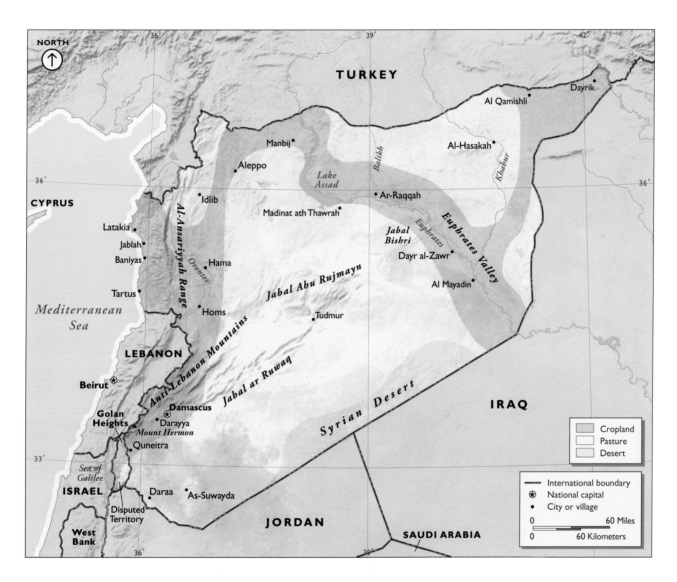

NORTH ↑

TURKEY

Dayrik

Al Qamishli

Manbij

Al-Hasakah

Aleppo

Balikh

Khabur

Lake Assad

CYPRUS

Idlib

Ar-Raqqah

Al-Ansariyyah Range

Madinat ath Thawrah

Jabal Bishri

Euphrates

Euphrates Valley

Latakia

Jablah

Orontes

Hama

Dayr al-Zawr

Baniyas

Jabal Abu Rujmayn

Tartus

Mediterranean Sea

Homs

Tudmur

Al Mayadin

IRAQ

Anti-Lebanon Mountains

Jabal ar Ruwaq

Syrian Desert

LEBANON

Beirut ✪

Golan Heights

Damascus ✪

Darayya

Mount Hermon

Quneitra

Sea of Galilee

ISRAEL

Daraa

As-Suwayda

Disputed Territory

JORDAN

SAUDI ARABIA

West Bank

	Cropland
	Pasture
	Desert

——— International boundary
✪ National capital
• City or village

0   60 Miles
0   60 Kilometers

Geography of Syria

SEA AND MOUNTAINS, VALLEYS AND RIVERS

Syria's Mediterranean coastline stretches 110 miles (180 km) between Turkey to the north and Lebanon to the south. Here, sandy beaches alternate with the rocky headlands of the adjacent Al-Ansariyyah mountain range. Citrus, vegetables, grains, and olives are grown in abundance in this important agricultural region. Though the coastal plain is just a few miles wide, it receives the country's most plentiful rainfall, attracting intense

THE EUPHRATES RIVER

The Euphrates River begins high in the mountains of Turkey, where most of its water originates as winter rain and snow. From there, the river winds down through Syria and into Iraq, where it unites with its twin, the Tigris River, and eventually flows into the Persian Gulf. The river's banks are studded with remnants of thousands of years of history, including stone monuments, castles, towers, and churches.

Competition for the precious water flow has strained relations between Turkey, Syria, and Iraq, and all three have erected massive dams in an effort to control the river's output. In Syria, the Tabqa Dam, approximately 30 miles (50 km) upriver from the town of Ar Raqqah, was completed in 1973. It created a huge reservoir some 50 miles (80 km) long and averaging five miles (8 km) wide behind the dam.[1] A hydroelectric power plant built on the dam in 1977 provides electricity to the region. The Euphrates's reduced flow below the dam is supplemented by the Balikh and Khabur Rivers and small seasonal streams called wadis.

The Orontes River provides important irrigation for Syria.

cultivation. Limestone mountains just east of this plain parallel the coastline and provide additional land for farming on their terraced hills. Rising above the terraces are steep, rugged peaks and some of Syria's remaining forests.

> In spring, the western slopes of coastal mountain ranges are carpeted with colorful wildflowers.

On the other side of the mountain range is the northern end of the Great Rift Valley that divides western and eastern Syria. Here, the Orontes River flows north from Lebanon, its irrigating waters providing Syria with a lush and fertile landscape. Syria's other major river, the 1,740-mile- (2,800 km) long Euphrates, is one of the Middle East's most celebrated rivers.[2] It originates in Turkey and flows diagonally southeastward across eastern Syria, where its water irrigates crops as it courses through the Syrian Desert. The Euphrates is Syria's most important water source and only navigable river, though only flat-bottomed boats can negotiate its shallow waters.

Farther south, dividing Syria and Lebanon, are the Anti-Lebanon Mountains. Between the two countries is Mount Hermon, the range's highest peak at 9,232 feet (2,814 m).[3] It is also Syria's highest point. Moving southwest, the Anti-Lebanon Mountains gradually diminish in height until they reach the Golan Heights, a disputed Syrian territory seized by Israel in 1967. This basalt plateau receives a significant amount of winter rainfall, making it an immensely important source of water to the region. For centuries, the Homs Gap, a pass between the Al-Ansariyyah and Anti-Lebanon ranges, has been a popular route for both peaceful traders and invaders intent on conquering the country's interior.

The southernmost area of Syria is perhaps the most visually striking. The Jabal ad Druze volcano lies on the Hauran Plateau, an elevated volcanic region covered in black basaltic lava. The plateau is often snow covered in winter, providing a stark contrast to the black rocks. Though it is largely treeless, the plain has very fertile soil, produced by the same volcanic eruptions that create mounds of flowing lava. This soil, combined with adequate rainfall, makes the plateau a productive agricultural region. Between lava flows are abundant fields of wheat.

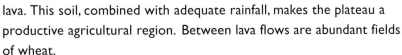

VOLCANIC ARCHITECTURE

The black basalt rocks left over from volcanic eruptions in the Hauran region were used in the area's distinctive architecture. The rocks feature in the black buildings of Bosra and in the black-and-white striped structures the Mamluks built during their reign in Syria between the twelfth and early sixteenth centuries.

DESERT AND STEPPE

Beginning on the eastern slopes of the Al-Ansariyyah and Anti-Lebanon ranges, eastern Syria is comprised of desert and high steppe. The

mountains form a natural barrier between east and west, preventing moisture from the sea from traveling inland. Thanks to this barrier, the eastern region is kept essentially dry. More than half of the country is covered by the Syrian Desert, a vast, mostly empty, semiarid expanse made up of sand in some areas and rock and gravel in others. Syria's capital city, Damascus, sits in the enormous Al-Ghuta Oasis, a verdant area of approximately 145 square miles (375 sq km) that separates the city from the Syrian steppe.[4] Its farms have provided the inhabitants of Damascus with cereals, vegetables, and fruits for thousands of years, enabling the city to prosper.

A squat chain of mountains divides the eastern plateau region. South of these mountains, a barren stony desert called the Hamad is notable for its spring sandstorms. These punishing storms damage vegetation and prevent grazing by the nomadic tribes that crisscross this region with herds of sheep and camels. In the southeast, the annual precipitation is less than four inches (10 cm).[5] Another barren area, the Homs Desert, lies east of the city of Homs.

CLIMATE

The climate of Syria is as variable as its geography. The coastal regions have a Mediterranean climate, with hot, humid summers and mild, rainy winters. In the mountains, summer heat is moderated by elevation,

Few people live in Syria's sandy, rocky deserts.

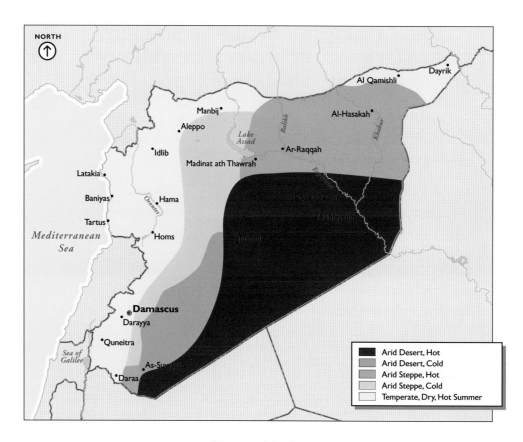

NORTH

Dayrik
Al Qamishli
Manbij
Aleppo
Lake Assad
Al-Hasakah
Balikh
Khabur
Idlib
Ar-Raqqah
Madinat ath Thawrah
Latakia
Dayr al-Zawr
Baniyas
Hama
Orontes
Al Mayadin
Tartus
Homs
Mediterranean Sea
Damascus
Darayya
Quneitra
Sea of Galilee
As-Suwayda
Daraa

⬛	Arid Desert, Hot
▨	Arid Desert, Cold
▧	Arid Steppe, Hot
▨	Arid Steppe, Cold
▢	Temperate, Dry, Hot Summer

Climate of Syria

AVERAGE TEMPERATURE AND PRECIPITATION

Region (City)	Average January Temperature Minimum/Maximum	Average July Temperature Minimum/Maximum	Average Precipitation January/July
Mediterranean Coastal Strip (Latakia)	48/58°F (9/14°C)	76/82°F (24/28°C)	6.4/0 inches (16/0 cm)
South Inland Region (Damascus)	33/53°F (6/12°C)	62/96°F (17/36°C)	1.5/0 inches (3.8/0 cm)
East Desert Region (Dayr al-Zawr)	38/52°F (3/11°C)	80/102°F (27/39°C)	1.2/0 inches (3/0 cm)[9]

but the winters are much more severe than in the coastal areas. The steppe and deserts see sizzling summers with average temperatures reaching 100 degrees Fahrenheit (38°C) or even 110 degrees Fahrenheit (43°C).[6] These extreme summer temperatures give way to winter temperatures that can dip below freezing. On the vast steppes and plains away from the coast, frost is common and snow is not unusual.

Rainfall averages approximately 30 inches (76 cm) per year on the coast, but the eastern regions receive much less.[7] The steppes receive between ten and 20 inches (25 and 51 cm) of precipitation, while the desert regions get only five inches (13 cm) or less.[8] Precipitation is unpredictable, and in dry years rainfall is reduced significantly.

CHAPTER 3

ANIMALS AND NATURE: AN ENVIRONMENT IN PERIL

Syria has no national animal, but an important symbol of the country is the hawk. A hawk is featured on Syria's coat of arms, and a sculpture of a hawk dating to the tenth millennium BCE was reportedly found by archaeologists in 2010. At least three different species of hawk live in Syria today.[1]

Syria's deserts and mountains are home to several species of large mammals, including hyenas, wolves, gazelles, jackals, and wild boar. Smaller mammals such as foxes, hares, weasels, and rodents are found throughout the region. The deserts still support snakes and other reptiles, including one gecko species that lives exclusively in

Lizards are common in the Syrian Desert and enjoy basking in the sun.

The northern goshawk is one of Syria's hawk species.

ENDANGERED SPECIES IN SYRIA

According to the International Union for Conservation of Nature (IUCN), Syria is home to the following numbers of species that are categorized by the organization as Critically Endangered, Endangered, or Vulnerable:

Mammals	16
Birds	14
Reptiles	6
Amphibians	0
Fishes	34
Mollusks	1
Other Invertebrates	7
Plants	3
Total	81[2]

the black basalt desert of eastern Syria. Desert oases also provide stopovers for migratory birds. But the number of threatened species is increasing, due largely to the increasing scarcity of water as a result of human activities and climate change. Some of the more critically endangered species are the northern bald ibis, the Nubian ibex, the Arabian oryx, the golden hamster, and the Mediterranean monk seal.

A wide array of plants can also be found within the country's borders. Hardy trees grow in mountainous regions, and flowers and grasses flourish in the springtime before withering

Scientists believe the last remaining group of Nubian ibexes in Syria is a small population in the Golan Heights.

SYRIAN TULIPS

Of the thousands of plant species indigenous to Syria, one of the most surprising is the wild tulip. While Holland is most commonly thought of as the tulip's homeland, the flower is actually indigenous to Syria.

under the summer sun. There are at least 3,700 known plant species in Syria.[3] By comparison, England and Germany have approximately 1,800 and 2,800, respectively.[4]

ENVIRONMENTAL CHALLENGES

In the distant past, Syria was home to a remarkable array of animal and plant life. Inscriptions in historic ruins and studies of ancient cities show that biodiversity was flourishing and abundant. Even as recently as the beginning of the twentieth century, travelers throughout Syria recorded seeing numerous species of fauna and flora that are today extinct. Some of the remarkable indigenous mammals that no longer exist in Syria include the lion, the Syrian brown bear, the Syrian tiger, and the Anatolian leopard. A magnificent flightless bird known as the Arabian ostrich once inhabited the semidesert regions.

Human habitation in Syria goes back thousands of years and includes some of the earliest civilizations on Earth. It has also taken a drastic toll on the region's animal and plant life. Agriculture has been both the lifeblood of the human settlements and the downfall of the environment.

Wetlands have been drained and forests felled for farmland. Lake water has been diverted for irrigation, leaving only small fishponds. Even the Euphrates River has been dammed up as a way of expanding arable land. Recently, the extensive use of agricultural chemicals has severely polluted the country's precious water supply. Further, the steppes have been overgrazed by herds of sheep, goats, donkeys, and camels, leaving little natural vegetation.

Signs of modest progress are visible. In an effort to turn the tide on Syria's substantial conservation problems, a number of organizations have sought to focus the nation's attention on its problems. In 2001, the Syrian Environmental Association was formed. This group has had significant success in outreach activities with schoolchildren, who enthusiastically engage with environmental issues. For the 2002 World Summit for Sustainable Development, the Syrian Ministry of State for Environmental Affairs adopted the Syrian National Environmental Action Plan, which targeted priority areas and created an environmental action plan for sustainable development.

RESTORING THE STEPPE

The Syrian Arab Republic's Badia steppe stretches across some 25 million acres (10 million ha) of the central and northeastern part of the country.[5] With poor soils and low rainfall, it is suitable only as grazing land. The Bedouin communities, some partially settled and some still nomadic, herd approximately 12 million sheep, goats, and camels in this area.[6] After many years of overgrazing and severe drought, the Badia became badly degraded, reduced in large areas to bare soil. For the Bedouin, their harsh life in the desert became even more difficult, with no vegetation left for their herds.

The International Fund for Agricultural Development, a specialized agency of the United Nations, is working with local communities to manage the rangelands. Rehabilitation has restored vegetation and helped reduce herders' vulnerability to drought and the effects of climate change. The project has also created employment opportunities for women in a region where there are few such prospects.

PRESERVING DIVERSITY

To date, Syria has established 23 protected areas, including wetlands, coastal and marine areas, forest areas, and a special bald ibis area. Most are closed to the public, but some, such as the al-Talila Nature Preserve near Palmyra and the al-Frunluq Nature Reserve in northwestern Syria, are open to visitors in an effort to foster greater environmental awareness.

Al-Talila aims to help visitors discover and interpret the biodiversity and ecosystems of the steppe and the links

Grazing by animals such as sheep has caused damage to Syria's environment.

between the daily lives of the local people and the natural world of the steppe. Two reintroduced species, the Arabian oryx and the sand gazelle, both of which had been locally extinct but are now making comebacks, can be seen in the area. Scientists' ultimate goal is to fully release them back into the wild. Syria hopes to duplicate this process with other species in other reserves, bringing the country back from the brink of ecological catastrophe.

SAVING WILD IBISES

Until April 2002, when an adult northern bald ibis was found on a remote cliff in the desert near Palmyra, the bird was thought to be extinct in the wild. Soon after, a total of four of these majestic creatures were found in Syria, making the ibis the most critically endangered bird in the region. Once revered as a symbol of brilliance and splendor, the ibis is now a sad symbol of terrible environmental damage. Saving the species will be an uphill battle.

Using satellite tagging to learn the ibis's migration route, researchers learned the bird travels through eight countries. They also discovered that young ibises die primarily from hunting or from flying into power lines. One juvenile bird they tracked was shot in northern Saudi Arabia on the very first day of its migration.

In 2008, there were fewer than a dozen northern bald ibises left in Syria.

CHAPTER 4

HISTORY: OLD LAND, YOUNG COUNTRY

Artifacts of human habitation in Syria date back as far as 200,000 years, during the Middle Paleolithic Period. From this time through the Mesolithic Period, people typically lived in hunter-gatherer societies. An abrupt cultural shift took place some 12,000 years ago with the founding of the earliest permanent agricultural settlements. Called the Neolithic Revolution by archaeologists, this transition essentially marks the beginning of civilization. Unlike the hunting-and-gathering existence, which required constant effort to survive, the agricultural life alternated between intense activity and leisure. As a result, society favored invention and advancement. The first real architecture was created, plants and animals were domesticated for reliable food sources, and pottery vessels were developed to store food. During the Ubaid period, between roughly 5500 and 4000 BCE, a settlement on the upper Euphrates River called Tell Zeidan flourished. At this time, irrigation became prevalent,

A gold plaque created by an ancient civilization in northeast Syria

THE LOST CITY

Tell Zeidan, a prehistoric town in what is now northern Syria, reveals remarkable clues about the development of ancient Middle Eastern societies, including the emergence of social inequality. Evidence indicates that the Ubaid civilization was among the first Near East cultures to have divided its population according to wealth and power. The wealthy utilized red stone seals to mark their most prized possessions. The stone is not local but rather comes from a region nearly 200 miles (322 km) to the east, showing that the wealthy residents of Tell Zeidan traveled long distances to secure the materials needed for many of their treasured artifacts.

long-distance trade grew in importance, centralized temples were built, political leaders rose to power, and social classes were established.

By approximately 2500 BCE, Syria was at the center of a vast Semitic empire. Damascus and Aleppo, the first true cities in Syria, developed at this time. The city of Ebla, southwest of Aleppo, was estimated to have had a population of 260,000 in 2500 BCE.[1] The language spoken there is believed to be the oldest Semitic language. The extensive writings of the Ebla culture give evidence of a vibrant culture akin to those of Mesopotamia and Egypt.

Ebla's reach spread north to Turkey and east to Mesopotamia, attracting the attention of Sargon of Akkad, a Babylonian warrior king.

An illustrated reconstruction of the city of Ebla

He led his armies up the Euphrates, destroying Ebla around 2250 BCE and incorporating the region into his empire. Sargon was the first notable conqueror of Syria.

CONQUESTS AND OCCUPATIONS

That first Babylonian invasion was a precursor to thousands of years of conquest and occupation. Around 1600 BCE, the Phoenicians developed an advanced, thriving civilization in the area that today makes up the Lebanese and Syrian coastal regions. Their successful trade and industry attracted successive invaders, including the Amorites, the Hittites, the Egyptians, and the group known as the Sea Peoples. The invaders devastated many of the settlements on the Mediterranean coast. The city of Ugarit was completely destroyed and would be abandoned forever. Simultaneously, the Arameans, an alliance of seminomadic Semitic tribes, slowly established trading routes into southwestern Asia, eventually creating the kingdom of Aram-Damascus.

The next civilization to conquer Syria was Assyria. While the vital and vibrant Assyrian culture was influencing societies as far away as Greece and Rome, its military was laying waste to cities, conquering Aram-Damascus in 732 BCE.

A stone depiction of the Assyrian king who conquered Aram-Damascus

The political situation continued to fluctuate, with the Assyrians being defeated by the Babylonians, who were in turn overthrown by the Persians in 539 BCE under Cyrus the Great. But the Persian Empire also collapsed, defeated in 333 BCE by perhaps the most illustrious conqueror in ancient history: Alexander the Great.

HELLENISTS, ROMANS, AND BYZANTINES

Alexander the Great ended Persia's nearly 200-year rule in Syria as part of his spectacular military campaign across Asia. Alexander did not live long after his triumph, but the Greek influence he spread lasted for centuries. Syrian and Greek cultures fused in the region, resulting in developments in law, philosophy, and science. Syrian trade vastly expanded, reaching deep into Asia and Europe. The Silk Road, established in approximately the first century BCE, made it much easier to exchange goods with China and the Far East.

The Silk Road was more than 4,000 miles (6,400 km) long.

The Greek presence eventually unraveled, and the Seleucids, who had broken away from Alexander's empire, seized control of the region. But by the first century BCE, Syria was again ripe for conquest. Rome, then a new world power, annexed Syria in 64 BCE, and the region finally stabilized. Roman control marked the beginning of greater prosperity for the country. Located at the western end of trade routes leading to the east, Syria was in the perfect position to supply the enormous Roman market with exotic and costly goods.

Alexander the Great died less than ten years after conquering Syria.

QUEEN ZENOBIA

The Roman ruins of Palmyra are among the most beautiful in all of Syria, an appropriate reminder of the woman who once ruled this colony. Queen Zenobia was the second wife of Udaynath, ruler of Palmyra in 260 CE. Following her husband's assassination seven years later, Zenobia took power. Ambitious and determined, she quickly rejected Roman rule and rallied her people. By 269, she had gained control of all of Syria and declared independence from the empire. Setting out to claim territories for herself, she first seized Egypt in 269 and then occupied Anatolia as far west as Ankara. In 271, Zenobia declared her son emperor.

Finally, the Romans fought back. Emperor Aurelian marched east to meet her, defeating her army under Zenobia's own command, first at Antioch and Emesa, then at besieged Palmyra. Sources differ about Zenobia's fate. According to some, she was captured, taken to Rome in gold chains, and beheaded. Others say she died on the way to Rome either from illness or from intentionally fasting herself to death. Palmyra itself was spared retaliation at first, but when the citizens revolted yet again in 273, the city was sacked.

In 193 CE, the marriage of a Roman emperor and the Syrian daughter of a high priest produced a dynasty of Syrian-born rulers more Eastern oriented than their European predecessors. Emperor Constantine I would emphasize this shift by moving the empire's capital eastward from Rome to his namesake city of Constantinople in 330.

ISLAM AND THE CALIPHATES

The force that ultimately ended Roman rule in Syria was religious rather than purely militaristic. In 630, the Prophet Muhammad and thousands of his followers marched on Mecca in modern-day Saudi

Arabia, taking the city and converting the residents to Islam. Muhammad's religious message rapidly gained adherents, and by his death in 632, most tribes of the Arabian Peninsula had converted to Islam. Many independent factions were united into a single religious entity.

After Muhammad's death, a new leader was sought. Ultimately the Umayyads, the strongest clan, won the power struggle. Conquering Syria in 636, they converted most of the populace to Islam, and Arabic gradually became the common language. The remaining Christians and Jews were tolerated, and some breakaway Christian sects received better treatment than they had under Byzantine rule, which was Orthodox Christian. Damascus became the capital of the Islamic world. The first major Islamic monuments were built by the Umayyads, including the Great Mosque in Damascus and the Dome of the Rock in Jerusalem.

The dynasty declined under later Umayyad caliphs. In 750, the Abbasids of northeast Iran overthrew the Umayyads and established their caliphate in Baghdad in present-day Iraq. Syria was no longer a dominant location in the Islamic world. But Abbasid rule was precarious. During this time, several religious sects branched off from mainstream Islam, including the Alawites and the Druze. Finally, the Seljuks, Turkish Muslims who had established a kingdom in Asia Minor, conquered northern Syria in 1055. By 1071, they had conquered all of Syria. Their intolerance toward

The Dome of the Rock was completed in approximately 692.

European Christians making pilgrimages to Palestine opened the door to Syria's next great threat.

THE CRUSADES

With the goal of freeing Christian holy places from Muslim rule, Pope Urban II declared the First Crusade in 1095. Some 150,000 soldiers, mostly Franks and Normans from Western Europe, traveled eastward and eventually captured much of the politically fragmented region, including the holy city of Jerusalem.[2] In their indiscriminate zeal, they slaughtered the residents at will, including Muslims, Jews, and Syrian Christians. Their barbarous acts prompted many local Christians to convert to Islam and join their fellow Syrians. The Crusaders built impenetrable hilltop fortresses, and by 1124 they occupied Antioch, Jerusalem, and the coastline. But the Crusaders maintained power only as long as the surrounding Muslim states were weak and divided.

In 1187, at the height of the Second Crusade, Salah al-Din Yusuf ibn Ayyub, commonly known in the West as Saladin, routed the Crusaders at the Battle of Hattin, retaking Jerusalem. Saladin soon recovered all of Palestine and most Crusader strongholds, apart from a few coastal towns. The Third Crusade, with the participation of England's legendary Richard the Lionheart, recaptured part of the coast, though Jerusalem remained in Muslim control. After wins and losses on both sides, a truce negotiated in

It is estimated that less than one-third of the Crusaders who left Europe survived the entire journey to Jerusalem.

1192 granted all pilgrims peaceful access to the Holy City. Richard sailed for Europe, never to return to the Holy Land. Saladin died in Damascus of malaria soon after.

THE MAMLUKS

Saladin's family, the Ayyubids, feuded over his territory after his death. Their squabbling proved beneficial to their cultural legacy: opposing princes competed to outdo one another architecturally, building glorious mosques, schools, and other public buildings. The Ayyubids were backed by a professional army, mainly of Turkish and Circassian origin, called the Mamluks. In 1250, when the last Ayyubid ruler died, a Mamluk named Baybars I al-Bunduqdari established himself as sultan of a reunited Syria and Egypt, beginning the 250-year-long Mamluk dynasty.

The next few years brought a rampaging invasion force like none ever seen before: the Mongols. Destroying everything and everyone in their path, the Mongols of Central Asia, led by a son of Genghis Khan, captured Baghdad before continuing west to Damascus and Palestine. The Mamluks finally stopped the invasion force in Syria in 1260. The Mongols invaded one final time in 1401, when they managed to reach Damascus. But their bid to retain the city failed, and they retreated back to Samarkand in Central Asia, burning cities and wiping out populations as they went.

The interior of a fortress built by the Mamluks in Syria

The Ottoman governor of Syria in 1917

THE OTTOMAN EMPIRE

In 1300, the Ottomans, nomadic Islamic Turks from central Asia, declared themselves the rightful heirs of the Seljuks and founded a principality in northwest Turkey. They soon began invading the surrounding areas. Little by little, they conquered all of the Middle East, including Syria by 1516.

Syria did not prosper under Ottoman rule. The population decreased drastically, and hundreds of villages disappeared. Still, as they had for centuries, European traders continued to transport spices, fruits, and textiles from the East back to the West via the Silk Road. By the fifteenth century, Aleppo was the region's chief marketplace, exceeding Damascus in wealth and furthering an ongoing rivalry between the two cities.

The Ottoman Empire was in decline by the nineteenth century. European powers, especially France and the United Kingdom, took advantage of Ottoman weakness through military, political, and economic means. When the Ottomans allied with the Germans in World War I (1914–1918), the stage was set for Syrian independence.

INDEPENDENCE AND UPRISING

By the end of World War I, Arab troops led by Faisal I and supported by British forces captured Damascus, ending four centuries of Ottoman rule. Following the defeat of Germany and the Ottoman Empire, Faisal promoted Arab self-rule of Syria at the 1919 peace conference in Versailles. Elections for a Syrian National Congress were held in 1920, and Faisal was declared king of Syria.

But Faisal's newly created Arab kingdom was soon divided. The 1920 San Remo Conference placed Syria under French command. When French forces occupied Damascus, Faisal fled abroad. He was then made king of Iraq by the British. Beginning in 1925, agitation against French rule turned into a nationwide uprising. In 1928, a national assembly drafted a constitution for Syria, but the French rejected the proposal, sparking further protests. The Franco-Syrian Treaty of Independence was signed in 1936, creating an independent Syrian nation. However, France still maintained military bases in the country.

In 1940, when France fell to Nazi German forces during World War II (1939–1945), Syria came under the control of the Nazi-controlled French government. A year later, British and French resistance troops invaded and occupied Syria, promising to allow free elections. The United States and United Kingdom recognized Syria's independence in 1944, but the French were slow to withdraw. In April 1946, the last French troops departed, and Syria became an independent nation again.

ONGOING STRUGGLES

During the 1950s, competing political factions vied for power. Hoping to reduce the political divisions, top military officers sought an alliance with Egypt. On February 1, 1958, Egypt and Syria announced the joining of the two countries as the United Arab Republic (UAR). But political decisions were primarily made in the Egyptian capital of Cairo, and Syrians grew to dislike the dominant Egyptian rule. A Syrian military coup in September 1961 removed the nation from Egyptian influence, and Syria seceded from the UAR, proclaiming itself the Syrian Arab Republic.

President Gamal Abdel Nasser of Egypt, *left*, and President Shukri al-Quwatli of Syria celebrate the union of their nations.

Instability quickly followed the nation's new birth, and in 1963 a group of army officers calling themselves the National Council of the Revolutionary Command seized power. They found a radical socialist government dominated by the Ba'ath Party, a secular Arab political group. More internal struggles followed. In the end, Defense Minister General Hafez al-Assad took power in a bloodless coup, assuming the presidency in March 1971.

Although Assad brought stability to the country, his regime was widely criticized for its harsh political repression and apparent support of international terrorism. Assad died of a heart attack in June 2000. A month later, a constitutional amendment lowered the presidential minimum age from 40 to 34, allowing Assad's 34-year-old son, Bashar, to assume the office.

Bashar al-Assad continued and worsened his father's political repression, and beginning in March 2011, demonstrations and unrest spread to nearly every city amid increasing calls for him to step down. Although the government granted some concessions, it also increased the use of deadly force against the

THE ALAWITES

The Assad family belongs to the Alawite minority, a Shia Muslim sect that cemented its control over the country when Hafez al-Assad rose to power. The sect was established in approximately 850 CE but for centuries held little power. Today, Alawite elites dominate the country's government and security forces. This power stems from their backing of the Ba'ath party at its inception in 1947. Most of Syria's military is Alawite.

The Assad family, including Hafez, *right front,* and Bashar, *second from left*

rising opposition. Through September 2012, it was estimated that more than 30,000 Syrians had been killed in the uprising.[3]

CHAPTER 5
PEOPLE: MIDDLE EAST MELTING POT

Arabs comprise 90 percent of the approximately 22 million Syrians.[1] Determining the demographics for the rest of the population can be difficult; while some minority groups are defined primarily by ethnicity, most identify themselves by religion. The remaining 10 percent of Syria's ethnic makeup includes Kurds, Assyrians/Syriacs, Druze, Armenians, Circassians, Aramaeans, Europeans, and Turks and Turkmens.[2] The religious makeup of the Syrian population is proportionately similar to the ethnic divisions: approximately three-quarters follow Sunni Islam, followed by Shia Islam, Druze (considered both an ethnic group and a religion), and Christians of various denominations, including Antiochian Orthodox, Greek Catholic, Assyrian Church of the East, Armenian Orthodox, and Protestants.[3]

Syrian Muslims pray in Damascus. Muslims make up 90 percent of Syria's population.

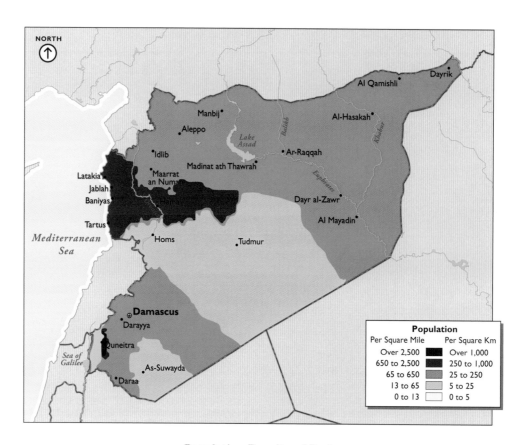

NORTH

Al Qamishli
Dayrik

Manbij

Aleppo

Idlib

Latakia
Jablah
Baniyas

Tartus

Mediterranean
Sea

Maarrat
an Numa

Madinat ath Thawrah

Hama

Homs

Lake
Assad

Balikh

Al-Hasakah

Khabur

Ar-Raqqah

Euphrates

Dayr al-Zawr

Al Mayadin

Tudmur

Damascus

Darayya

Quneitra

Sea of
Galilee

As-Suwayda

Daraa

Population

Per Square Mile		Per Square Km
Over 2,500		Over 1,000
650 to 2,500		250 to 1,000
65 to 650		25 to 250
13 to 65		5 to 25
0 to 13		0 to 5

Population Density of Syria

The population of Syria is extremely young, with a median age of 22.3 in 2012. By comparison, the median age in the United States in 2012 was 37.1.[4] This statistic may have a profound effect on the country's political future, given the increasing hostility of the young toward the Assad regime. By 2012, 56 percent of Syrians lived in cities, with much of the rural-to-city movement occurring in Damascus.[5] As a result of this movement, valuable farmland is shrinking, pollution and traffic are worsening, and precious water is being depleted. With many older buildings being demolished, new residents are often forced to live in substandard homes where conveniences such as electricity and running water are rare.

POPULATION DIVERSITY

The Arab presence in Syria dates to the Roman period. By the time of the Islamic conquest, Syrians were already identifying themselves as Arabs and speaking Arabic. Some Arab minorities, such as the nomadic Bedouin, who travel through the desert and steppe and herd sheep, live isolated from other groups. Palestinian refugees, driven from their homeland in 1948 after the founding of Israel, typically live either in working-class neighborhoods in Damascus or in refugee camps.

Approximately 500,000 Palestinians live in Syria.

Nearly 2 million Kurds, mostly Sunni Muslims, form Syria's largest ethnic minority.[6] Most prefer speaking their Indo-European language, Kurdish, though many also know

Arabic. The Kurds have resisted assimilation, living northeast of Aleppo, along the Turkish border, and on the outskirts of Damascus. Fiercely independent, the Kurds are traditionally nomadic herders. Many can trace their ancestors in Syria back to the sixth century BCE, though some came from Turkey in the 1920s and 1930s when the Turkish government cast them out. A small number of ethnic Kurds called Yazidi practice a dualist religion, believing that evil and good are both parts of divinity, and the devil should be shown deep fear and respect. One Yazidi community in the Afrin valley in northwest Syria dates back at least to the twelfth century.

Armenians form Syria's second-largest ethnic minority and its most prominent Christian group—Armenians were among the first converts to Christianity. Many live in or near Aleppo, where they have been since the fourth century, but most arrived after World War I, fleeing from the Ottoman Empire's slaughter of hundreds of thousands of Armenians.[7]

LANGUAGES

Most Syrians speak Arabic, and it is the country's official language. Other tongues heard in Syria include Kurdish, Armenian, Turkish, Turkmen, and Adyghian (the language of Circassians), as well as some English and French. But on the eastern slopes of the Anti-Lebanon Mountains north of Damascus, in a cluster of Christian villages, Aramaic—the

A young Syrian girl participates in a protest in 2012. Syria's very young population may significantly impact the nation's future.

YOU SAY IT!

English	Arabic (Levantine)
Hello	Marhaban (MAR-hah-ban)
Good-bye	Ma' as-salaameh (MAH-sah-lah-meh)
Yes	Na'am (NAHM)
No	Laa (LEH)
Thank you	Shukran (SHOO-kran)
You're welcome	A'afwan (AH-fwahn)

language of Jesus and his disciples—is still spoken. Recognized as an endangered language, Aramaic, also called Western Neo-Aramaic, is spoken by 7,000 people in the town of Ma'alula.[8] Most of these speakers are Greek Catholics whose churches and rites long predate the arrival of Islam and Arabic. In two nearby villages, one of which is entirely Muslim, an additional 8,000 people also speak this ancient language.[9]

Previously isolated because of their location, these villages have not only come into contact with the outside world, but have even become tourist destinations because of their unique linguistic character. However, this exposure also threatens the continued survival of the language. Rather than let the language die off, the Aramaic Language Academy, part of the University of Damascus, was created to teach, preserve, and revive Western Neo-Aramaic. Experts believe this ancient language probably still sounds much the same as it did more than 2,000 years ago.

The Aramaic language dates back to 800 BCE.

OTHER MINORITY ETHNIC GROUPS

Turks and Turkmen have lived in Syria dating back to the Seljuk conquest in 1055 CE. For the most part, Turks live in cities and towns in northern Syria, including Aleppo. This strong sense of ethnic identity has imparted a distinct Turkish flavor to much of northern Syria. Approximately half of the Turkmen living in Syria today speak Turkmen, a Turkic language linguistically close to Turkish.[10]

Though they spoke Neo-Aramaic, Assyrian refugees arriving from Iraq in the 1930s quickly assimilated when they relocated to Syrian cities

and intermarried. Assyrians live all across the country but principally in the east. More refugees came from Iraq after the United States invaded the country in 2003.

Several thousand Circassians, descendants of refugees who fled the Russian invasion of the North Caucasus in the late nineteenth century, live mostly in Damascus. The Ottomans initially settled the refugee Circassians on Bedouin tribal land, leading to conflict and raids by the Bedouin. The Circassians prevailed and established their own communities.

RELIGION IN SYRIA

Syria has a long history of religious tolerance, and freedom of worship is guaranteed in the Syrian constitution. Still, Syrians tend to identify primarily with their religious group or sect. Because three-quarters of the population are Sunni Muslims, this creates a strong feeling of cultural unity.[11] The remaining Syrians have different religious practices, many being offshoots of the Shia branch of Islam.

The Alawite branch of Shia Islam is Syria's largest religious minority. Most live in northwestern Syria, in the

> Traditional Alawites do not allow women to attend religious gatherings.

Syrian Assyrians reenact an ancient wedding ceremony in celebration of the Assyrian New Year.

mountains overlooking the Mediterranean and on the coast itself, though some make their home on the inland plains of Homs and Hama. The Alawite community has maintained itself for more than a millennium, surviving repeated persecutions by the Sunni majority. Alawites hold religious observances in private homes, and their festivals include Persian and Christian holy days. For centuries, Alawites lived in poverty on the fringes of society, but this changed after Syrian statehood. The Alawites embraced the Ba'ath Party and rose to power with it. In 1971, Hafez al-Assad became the first Alawite president of Syria. His son Bashar is also Alawite.

Identified as a separate ethnic group in Syria primarily because of their distinctive religion, the Druze are ethnically a combination of Arab and Aramaic ancestry. They dominate in the mountainous region of southern Syria and the town of Suweida. The Druze combine various Jewish, Christian, and Iranian elements under a doctrine of strict monotheism. Many of their religious practices are so secret that even members of the sect are kept in the dark about them. Only a select few, approximately 20 percent of the Druze population, are allowed to take part in the services and are permitted to learn the full Druze religious doctrine, the *hikmah*.[12] The Druze permit no conversions from or to their religion; intermarriage is also banned.

> The Druze believe a person can be reincarnated.

Christians have been in Syria almost since the religion's founding. During the Byzantine period, the ruling families of Syria were Christian

A Syrian Druze family plays in the snow.

Arabs loyal to Byzantium. Many of today's Syrians are descended from these families. Approximately 10 percent of the modern population is Christian.[13] Denominations include Greek Orthodox and Greek

Catholics, concentrated in and around Damascus, Latakiya, and the neighboring coastal region. Syriac Orthodox Christians live mainly in Homs, Aleppo, and Damascus. Syrian Catholics make their homes in small communities found in Aleppo, Hasaka, and Damascus. Finally, a small group of Maronite Christians lives mainly in the Aleppo region, a surviving remnant that has maintained ties to the Roman Catholic Church since the twelfth century and whose liturgy is in the ancient Syriac language.

There is also a very small population of Jews in Syria. The Jewish presence

PERSECUTION OF JEWS IN SYRIA

In 1946, when Syria gained independence, attacks on remaining Jewish citizens multiplied. On November 30, 1947, a day after the United Nations voted to partition Palestine into separate Arab and Jewish states, mobs pillaged Jewish neighborhoods, looting houses and burning synagogues. The government declared Jews enemies of Syria, and persecution became commonplace. Jews were forbidden to own property, travel, or practice their occupations, and any who tried to escape were incarcerated, tortured, and had their homes and property confiscated. Syrian Jews were held hostage by the government for decades. Finally in 1992, after vigorous campaigning by human rights organizations and American political leaders, the Assad regime permitted Jews to leave, and rescue efforts were quickly organized. Today, of a population that numbered around 40,000 before Israel's establishment, a mere handful of Jews remain living in Damascus, declining to leave what has always been their homeland.[14]

Syrian Orthodox Christians celebrate a baptism ceremony in 2012.

in Syria dates back to biblical times. According to tradition, the patriarch Abraham briefly settled in Aleppo in the second millennium BCE, when the city was part of the extended area of Israel, and the city's Great Synagogue was constructed in approximately 950 BCE, during King David's reign. Over the millennia, the situation for Jews varied, depending on the enactment or elimination of restrictive laws. During the Spanish Inquisition, when Jews fled Spain, many found refuge in Syria. They were welcomed by the Ottoman rulers, who believed the Jews would inspire trade and encourage economic growth. When the Ottomans lost their empire just prior to World War I, many Syrian Jews emigrated, mostly to North and South America.

It is estimated that only 100 Jews remain in Syria.

CHAPTER 6

CULTURE: ANCIENT INFLUENCES AND MODERN IDEAS

Syria's cultural history is as old as Syrian society, and its artistic, inventive, and philosophical achievements have enhanced and enriched the many civilizations that conquered the region over the ages. During the Greek and Roman eras, Syrian scholars and artists significantly contributed to Hellenistic and Roman philosophy and culture. Syrian and Greek cultures fused to create notable developments in philosophy, science, and law. Syrian and Mesopotamian deities and Greek and Roman gods merged. Subsequently, Greek and Roman religion and religious art adopted Syrian characteristics. But no empire left a more permanent mark than the Umayyads, who brought Islam to Syria in the seventh century.

Umayyad influences can still be seen in modern Syria, such as in the Great Mosque in Damascus.

ARTS AND CRAFTS

Traditional Syrian crafts were created for mostly functional purposes, but their sheer beauty can obscure this fact. Ivory carving from thousands of years ago produced objects as varied as furniture, drinking cups, and plaques. Syria embraced mosaic tile floors from the Romans, who were masters of this art. Each territory developed its own regional style, but in general the mosaic floors of Roman Syria were characterized by lush colors, mythological or figurative scenes, and architecturally inspired motifs.

Throughout the Byzantine and early Islamic periods, Syria became one of the greatest cultural centers in the Mediterranean. One striking example of this cultural output is Syrian metalwork. During the Crusades, Syrian swords and knives rose to prominence, and the European invaders feared the thin, curved blades with their reputation for sharpness, strength, and flexibility. The type of steel produced in Syria became known as Damascus steel. Handmade boxes, candlesticks, and plates made of copper, silver, and brass found their way to many homes in the West between the thirteenth and sixteenth centuries. These, along with copper and brass trays and samovars, can still be found in the souqs—although many of them found today are mass-produced knockoffs rather than traditional handcrafted examples.

Knowledge of the exact method used to make Damascus steel was lost in the eighteenth century.

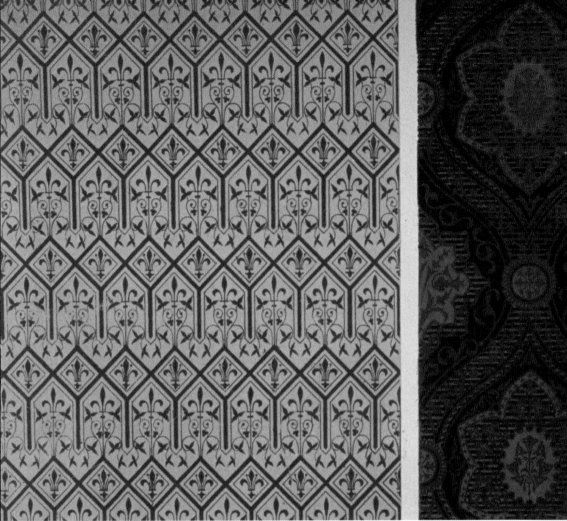

Crusaders introduced Damask fabric to Europe in the eleventh century.

Fabric arts have a long tradition in Syria. Damask, a lustrous cloth often made of silk and woven with intricate raised patterns, originated in Damascus and takes its name from the city. The traditional craft of

Jewish, Christian, and Muslim texts hold that Damascus took its name from two Semitic words, *dam,* or "blood," and *shaq,* or "spill," referencing the biblical story of the murder of Abel by his brother, Cain. According to legend, Cain's tomb is just west of the city.

embroidery has also been handed down through generations of Syrian women, whose complex, colorful designs transform simple garments and home furnishings into elaborate works of art.

Syrians also perfected the craft of intarsia, a woodworking technique similar to inlay but usually using bits of bone and mother-of-pearl to create striking white-on-wood designs. Wooden objects such as dressers, tables, and small trinket boxes employ intarsia, the designs most often depicting flowers and birds and other representations of nature or geometric shapes.

ARCHITECTURE, THEN AND NOW

In Syria, one can view architecture in an astounding array of forms, including cave dwellings, Mesopotamian palaces, Greek and Roman temples, Crusader castles, Byzantine churches, Islamic mosques, and even Bedouin tents. But Syrian architecture is most beautifully expressed

A mosaic in Syria's Sayyida Ruqayya mosque

in the nation's mosques. Mosque architecture evolved in Syria, notably including the eighth-century construction of the Great Umayyad Mosque in Damascus. Its vast courtyard dazzles visitors with polished white paving stones. The site of the Great Mosque had previously been a temple to the ancient Middle Eastern god Ba'al, then a Roman temple for their god Jupiter, and finally the Christian Church of Saint John the Baptist. The mosque was then built over this church.

Private dwellings also frequently incorporate courtyards in their designs. Many older urban homes feature interior courtyards complete with gardens and central fountains. Often, the structures' stark exterior walls display no hint of the tranquil havens within.

Village architecture has distinctive regional styles. Near the borders of Iraq and Turkey, conical mud-brick buildings resemble beehives, an architectural style dating back 1,000 years. Farther east, the mud-brick houses are built into large squares around a central courtyard used primarily for work rather than relaxation. A more primitive form of housing is the Bedouin tent. Traditional tents are made of black goat-hair panels sewn into a large rectangular shape.

The old houses in Damascus are different in construction from their contemporary counterparts. Whereas dwellings once were built of

The grid-patterned streets found in Syrian cities owe their style to the Greeks and Romans.

Courtyards have been common features of homes in the Middle East for thousands of years.

unbaked bricks, wood, and stone, modern buildings are built of concrete, which imparts a drab look to many homes. Government buildings, mosques, and churches are constructed of hewn stone, a building technique reserved solely for these structures.

POETRY AND LITERATURE

Since antiquity, Syrians have had a proud tradition of literature and poetry. Some of the oldest literary texts in Semitic languages have been unearthed at the ancient cities of Mari, Ebla, and Ugarit. During the Umayyad period, three Bedouin poets, al-Akhtal, al-Farazdaq, and Jarir, all born around 640, gained great fame and were favored by the rulers. Al-Mutanabbi, considered by many to be the last great classical Arab poet, was born in Iraq in 915.

Not until the Arab cultural revival of the nineteenth century did Syrian writers again rise in importance. One of the major Syrian

Syrian poet Adonis has been called the greatest living poet in the Arab world.

figures of this revival was the writer and poet Francis Marrash, whose 1856 work *Ghabat al-haqq* was among the first Arabic novels. However, contemporary writing is closely monitored, and authors, particularly of nonfiction, often face government censorship. Prominent contemporary Syrian writers include Adonis, an outspoken poet jailed and exiled to Lebanon for his political writings, Muhammad al-Maghout, a playwright whose works examine injustice and authoritarian governments, Nizar Qabbani, a poet who addresses political and social themes, and Ghada al-Samman, a popular Arab feminist author.

Islam prohibits images of religious figures, so mosque designers instead use intricate geometric and floral shapes.

MEDIA

The history of Syrian cinema dates back to the 1928 film *al-Muttaham al-Bari'* (*The Innocent Victim*), but the film industry in Syria today is tentative at best. Most commercially shown films are imports, coming from such places as Egypt and the United States. Given their often-meager earnings, many Syrian movie fans seeking good films prefer to watch pirated movies and DVDs.

Television, on the other hand, is beamed via satellite into most urban homes. There are two state-run channels, one of which shows foreign programming. But satellite TV also gives Syrians access to broadcasts that are not censored by the government, such the Arabic and English news channels.

In most countries, the Internet is now the primary source of information among the young, and Syria is no different. Although government interference and censorship are routine, attempts to control

A Syrian man uses a computer at an Internet café in Damascus.

access and censor information often fail. The government sometimes allows access to previously blocked Web sites such as YouTube, Amazon.com, and Facebook in order to monitor usage by opposition movements.

LEISURE TIME

Syrians make the most of their available leisure time. They love food, and as the hundreds of restaurants attest, eating out—whether at a fast-food shawarma stand, an outdoor café, or an upscale restaurant that offers live music with its dinners—is a regular pleasure. Weekend family picnics are also enjoyed, especially by city dwellers, for a chance to escape into nature and hear birdsong instead of the noises of the city.

Music is another source of pleasure, from Lebanese- and Indian-style pop to folk to classical Arabic and Western music, and performances are always well attended.

SYRIAN HOLIDAYS

In addition to standard Christian and Muslim holidays, notable holidays in Syria include the March 8 Revolution, which celebrates the Ba'ath Party's 1963 rise to power. Evacuation Day, on April 17, commemorates the exit of the last French troops from Syria in 1946. Martyrs' Day, on May 6, is held in remembrance of Syrian and Lebanese nationalists executed by Ottoman Empire officials in 1916.

A man prepares food at a shawarma stand in northern Syria.

Also enjoyed are a soak in a hammam, or bathhouse, and a good souq for shopping.

Rarely, though, is leisure time spent playing sports. Although Syrians passionately watch soccer, and kids will happily kick a ball around in the street for hours, participatory sports are not commonplace. The idea of enjoying athletic activities to keep fit is on the rise but hardly widespread, though weight lifting, judo, and karate are popular in the cities. Syria sent ten athletes to the 2012 Summer Olympics in London, England. They competed in boxing, swimming, and show jumping, among other events. They did not win any medals.

Ahmad Saber Hamcho and his horse Wonderboy competed for Syria in the show jumping competition at the 2012 Summer Olympics.

CHAPTER 7

POLITICS: A COUNTRY IN UPHEAVAL

On April 17, 1946, Syria's autonomy was finally established. But the decades following independence were as turbulent as the ones leading up to it, with competing factions fighting for political control. Syria endured a series of military coups that undermined civilian rule, ultimately leading to the seizure of power in 1951 by Colonel Adib Shishakli, who named

THE SYRIAN FLAG

Syria's flag features three horizontal stripes of equal size. From top to bottom, they are red, white, and black. Within the white stripe are two green stars, each having five points. The flag was adopted in 1980, though it is identical to the flag used by the short-lived United Arab Republic. The green stars represented the two member states of Syria and Egypt.

The Syrian flag

himself president. Shishakli was overthrown in 1954 in another coup, and maneuvering by various military groups resulted in a surge of Arab nationalists and socialist movements. A brief union between Syria and Egypt quickly disintegrated following Syrian dissatisfaction over Egyptian domination, and on September 28, 1961, Syria reestablished itself as the Syrian Arab Republic.

More instability ensued, leading to frequent changes of government. Then, on March 8, 1963, the Arab Socialist Resurrection Party, also known as the Ba'ath Party, engineered another coup. The National Council of the Revolutionary Command, a group of military and civilian officials, was installed, assuming control of all executive and legislative authority. Often called the Ba'ath Revolution, the change resulted in a radical secular-socialist government dominated by the Ba'ath Party, defining the future of Syria for decades to come.

The Iraqi dictator Saddam Hussein was a leading member of the Ba'ath Party.

THE BA'ATH PARTY AND SECULARISM

Syria is one of the most secular countries in the Arab world, and it has no official state religion. With the installation of the Ba'ath Party as the main political force in Syria, the country's secularism was firmly entrenched.

A Ba'ath Party conference was held in Damascus in 2000.

For many years, the Ba'ath regime in Syria has served as a significant force of secularism in the Middle East.

The Ba'ath Party's main ideological objectives are secularism, socialism, and pan-Arab unionism. In the place of Islam, the regime offers Arabism, a secular form of devotion to Arab interests, culture, aspirations, or ideals. When the Ba'ath Party rose to power, Arabism essentially served as the state religion; Islam was marginalized.

In Arabic, ba'ath means "renaissance."

But while the ruling Ba'ath Party professes a secular, pan-Arab socialism, the Sunni majority have long resented what they see as sectarian rule by the Alawites. The Alawites are Shia Muslims and make up only 12 percent of the population, but they are disproportionately represented in the security forces and other government jobs as a result of their personal and family connections to the ruling regime.[1] One of the main challenges faced by the opponents of the Assad regime is to reassure Alawites and the international community that there will be equality for all citizens in a post-Assad Syria.

SYRIAN GOVERNMENT

Syria's 1973 Constitution proclaims the virtues of freedom of expression and legal equality, but in practice these are generally ignored by the Assad regime. Formally, the government is made up of three branches: executive, legislative, and judicial.

STRUCTURE OF THE GOVERNMENT OF SYRIA

Executive Branch	Legislative Branch	Judicial Branch
President Vice Presidents Prime Minister Cabinet	People's Assembly	Supreme Judicial Council Supreme Constitutional Court

The executive branch is led by Syria's head of state, the president. The president is chosen by popular vote to serve a seven-year term. The president is aided by two vice presidents that handle specialized areas of governing, as well as a cabinet. The head of government is the prime minister. The president appoints people to all of these positions.

The legislative branch consists of one lawmaking body, the People's Assembly. A total of 250 members are elected to four-year terms by popular vote. Members are selected by voters within the region they represent. Until 2012, only members of the Ba'ath party or its affiliates could hold office. Under the new constitution, other parties are permitted to exist within Syria. The Assembly appoints presidential candidates, who are then subjected to a popular vote.

The judicial branch includes the Supreme Judicial Council, which appoints and removes judges. The president heads this council. At the national level, there is also the Supreme Constitutional Court, whose judges are appointed to four-year terms by the president. An appeals court known as the Court of Cassation and other appeals courts handle appeals at the national level. Specialized courts handle local disputes, dealing with juvenile, economic, and religious crimes.

The State Security Court is maintained solely for the purpose of trying political dissidents.

In 2012, Syria's president was Bashar al-Assad. Elevated to the office following his father's death in 2000, Assad was initially predicted to be a more liberal ruler, particularly with regard to economic reforms. He was reelected in 2007. However, Bashar proved to simply be a younger version of his iron-fisted father, escalating violence against protestors in 2011 and 2012. Prime minister Riyad Farid Hijab, former minister of agriculture, assumed office in June 2012. Only a few months later, in early August, he defected and joined the resistance movement.

REACHING THE BREAKING POINT

On the heels of revolutionary movements in other Middle Eastern countries, Syrian protests against the Assad regime's repressive policies,

Bashar al-Assad in 2009

widespread corruption, and unsound economic practices increased in early 2011. In March 2011, a group of teenagers in the southern city of Daraa were arrested and brutally tortured for spray painting the walls of their school with revolutionary slogans. Security forces opened fire during a march protesting the arrests, killing four.[2] In response to increased tensions, Syrian security forces sealed off the city.

These actions sparked nationwide pro-democracy demonstrations, igniting an ongoing cycle of protests met by government retaliation, primarily by the

AN ALAWITE VOICE OF OPPOSITION

Actress Fadwa Suleiman is a member of the Alawite sect. Unlike most of the Alawite elite, Suleiman is an outspoken dissident. At first, she only attended protests, but later she spoke at demonstrations in the city of Homs, a center of antigovernment resistance.

She played no part in the early demonstrations that broke out in March 2011, but disillusioned by the regime's control of theater and film, she was drawn to the protests. She had chosen to study theater because to her theater meant "freedom to think and to express oneself."[3] But she quickly discovered that theater, like most culture in Syria, is controlled by the state:

> I became opposed to the way we work, to the humiliation, the degradation in human interaction. Everywhere you go, even a theater or a film company, you feel you have entered a security branch. Authors write the worst scripts but they are chosen because they have links to security.[4]

Syrian security forces patrolled the city of Daraa in March 2011.

Sunni majority that has suffered the most under Assad's rule. From Daraa, demonstrations calling for the overthrow of Assad spread to the Kurdish northeast, to the coastal Latakia area, and to cities including Hama, Homs, Aleppo, and Damascus. The regime made some concessions, including the creation of a new constitution which allowed new political parties to form and which limited the term of office of the president.

> Bashar is also the commander in chief of the armed forces.

However, the regime cracked down on protestors with brutality, arresting and torturing hundreds of people, cutting off water and electricity to the most rebellious areas, and bombing cities and neighborhoods. But the protests continued unabated, and the government responded with increasing escalation. By October 2012, international observers estimated some 30,000 people had been killed.[5] Bashar al-Assad remained in power and continued to wage war against his people.

Protests increased in frequency and intensity in 2012.

CHAPTER 8

ECONOMICS: CRUDE OIL TO OLIVE OIL

Syria is a middle-income developing country whose economy has been based mostly on oil, agriculture, tourism, and industry. State-controlled businesses export wheat, cotton fiber, crude oil and petroleum products, fruits and vegetables, textiles and clothing, and meat and live animals. The country also has substantial deposits of phosphate, a mineral in demand as a fertilizer. Compared to many of its neighbors, whose economies are completely dependent on oil production, the Syrian economy is relatively diverse.

Until recently, Syria was nearly self-sufficient, producing the fundamental food needs of its own population. However, Syria's inefficient and corrupt centrally planned economy began facing serious challenges to growth even prior to the 2011 uprising. A bloated and poorly performing public sector, declining oil production, increasing deficit, weak financial

The Damascus lights are seen at night. Syria was once a relatively prosperous nation with a diverse economy.

TOURISM

Before the crisis, tourism in Syria was a reliable industry. Arabs, Europeans, and a handful of Americans visited Syria's beautiful, ancient cities, astonishing ruins, and Mediterranean resorts. They brought much-needed income to poor areas. But the violent turmoil has completely halted the industry, stopping the flow of tourist money into Syria. Many of the ancient wonders of Syria are in danger of being destroyed by bombs and shelling.

and capital markets, and high unemployment tied to high population growth have taken a drastic toll on both investment and productivity.

ECONOMIC SANCTIONS

In addition to internal fiscal challenges, Syria faces external economic woes. The United States imposed sanctions in 2004 for Syria's support of terrorism, its involvement in Lebanon, its weapons of mass destruction programs, and its destabilizing role in Iraq. Subsequent sanctions were levied in response to terrorist money-laundering, programs to develop weapons of mass destruction, and public corruption. Sanctions included restricting exports, denying access to funds deposited in US banks, and banning US corporations from involvement in Syria's oil industry.

In April 2011, in response to the Assad regime's brutality against dissidents, the United States imposed additional sanctions. The European

The United Nations Security Council discussed the prospect of economic sanctions against Syria in July 2012.

Union, Japan, Canada, and other countries have also implemented a range of sanctions on the Syrian government. Another significant economic blow was dealt in November 2011 when the Arab League severed trade and investment connections to Syria and suspended Syria's membership in the league. Aimed at stopping Syria's use of lethal force against protestors, this unprecedented step against a member state further weakened Syria's ties to its allies in the Arab world.

NATIONALISM AND PRIVATIZATION

The Assad regime introduced modest economic reforms in the first decade of the twenty-first century. The changes in Syria's economic system, intending to change the basic structure of businesses from state owned to privately owned, was a plan that ran counter to decades of nationalized ownership. When the Ba'ath Party took command of Syria in 1963, its Alawite leaders, citing socialist ideology, imposed centralized control of the economy. All utilities, heavy industry, and transportation were, and continue to be, government owned and operated. Farmers, artisans, tradespeople, and professionals were allowed to maintain independent businesses, though state-imposed controls reduced the incomes of farmers, merchants, and even physicians and other professionals. As a result of these policies, Syria failed to join an increasingly interconnected global economy. When Bashar al-Assad ascended to the presidency in 2000, he quickly promised more freedom and opportunity in the private sector. The government elite grumbled, but many Syrians felt a newfound optimism.

Assad followed through on some promises and relaxed some restrictions. In 2004, private banks were allowed to open for the first time. In 2009, a modest stock market was established, where wealthy Syrians could buy shares in a small number of companies, mostly banks and insurance firms. But despite these efforts, Syria's inefficient and corrupt centrally planned policies remain. The economy continues to be slowed by poorly performing public sector firms, low rates of investment, low productivity in both the industrial and agricultural sectors, and reduced domestic consumption. Instead of growth, the economy has recently seen a steady decline, fueling frustration among Syrians. Harsh sanctions have further worsened the economic picture. For these reasons, the conservative elite have argued that the privatization reforms have been a failure.

CENTRALLY PLANNED ECONOMIES

The Assad government operates what is called a centrally planned economy, a type of economy in which the state makes most production decisions for the country. It differs from a market economy, in which production decisions are made between consumers and businesses. A centrally planned economy uses state-owned companies to control what is produced and which resources are used in that production.

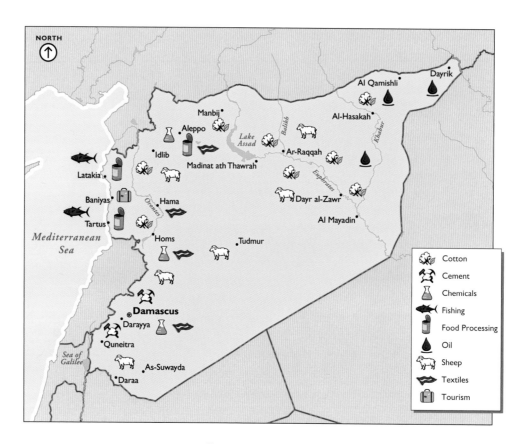

NORTH

Dayrik

Al Qamishli

Al-Hasakah

Manbij

Aleppo

Lake
Assad

Idlib

Ar-Raqqah

Madinat ath Thawrah

Latakia

Dayr al-Zawr

Baniyas

Hama

Tartus

Al Mayadin

Mediterranean
Sea

Homs

Tudmur

Damascus

Darayya

Quneitra

Sea of
Galilee

As-Suwayda

Daraa

	Cotton
	Cement
	Chemicals
	Fishing
	Food Processing
	Oil
	Sheep
	Textiles
	Tourism

Resources of Syria

AGRICULTURE AND INDUSTRY

In the 1970s, approximately 50 percent of Syria's population worked in agriculture.[1] By the 1980s that figure was down to 30 percent.[2] The 2011 figure was just 17 percent, contributing 16.9 percent of the gross domestic product (GDP) compared to approximately 25 percent only a few years prior.[3] Pressure on water supplies caused by heavy agricultural use, rapid population growth, industrial expansion, and water pollution was further increased by a severe multiyear drought.

A bright spot in Syria's badly damaged agricultural sector is its production of olive oil, which hit an all-time high of 200,000 short tons (181,000 metric tons) in 2011.[4] Though the months of turmoil have taken a hard toll on Syria's economy, olive-based products have been unscathed. However, much of the rest of the agriculture sector has been unable to match this performance. Farmers and agricultural workers have moved to crowded urban slums or to poor cities, flashpoints for the 2011 uprisings. While

WATER

A lack of water is among the most crucial problems Syria's agricultural sector faces. Grain production requires sufficient rainfall, and a drought lasting from 2006 to 2011 destroyed the livelihoods of thousands of small farmers and herders, forcing them to move from their land to the outskirts of western cities. Rainfall is supplemented with irrigation in dry years, but running the necessary water pumps places demands on electricity and diesel reserves, compounding the problem.

grain and other food products are not subject to international sanctions, because the sanctions are meant to target the Assad regime rather than the Syrian people, foreign banks, shippers, and traders are discouraged from doing business with Damascus.

Another pillar of the Syrian economy, crude oil, is faring even worse. When the sanctions were imposed, revenue to the Syrian government fell $4 billion by January 2012.[5] So far, the sanctions have hurt private citizens the hardest. The unemployment rate rose from 8.3 percent to 12.3 percent between 2010 and 2011.[6] Many Syrian youth have chosen to leave the country rather than attempt to navigate the chaotic situation there. Tens of thousands have left since the unrest, fleeing to neighboring countries not just for jobs but often for their lives.

A CURRENCY IN CRISIS

Syria's currency is the Syrian pound; it was introduced in 1919 when the country was still under French control. The colorful banknotes feature images of notable Syrians and of Syrian architecture. The currency shed its value by 45 percent against the US dollar and the euro in the year following the start of the 2011 uprising.[7] This drop adds to the economic woes of the Syrian people, whose cost of living increases with instability. The stock market has witnessed a 40 percent drop since the beginning of the conflict, and personal bank deposits have fallen

Syria has been commercially producing oil since the 1960s.

by 35 percent.[8] Economists forecasted the economy would shrink by 5.9 percent in 2012.[9]

The battle against the growing insurgency drained the government's coffers, and Syrian officials called upon Iran, their closest ally, for money. But Iran had its own economic woes, and its financial support was limited. Nonetheless, it appeared unlikely that Assad and his closest associates would suffer as a result of the sanctions and embargoes that are hurting the rest of the population. It was believed that Assad had financial reserves and a sizable black-market income that would make it easier for him to maintain his grip on power.

Syrian banknotes

CHAPTER 9

SYRIA TODAY

As in many societies, politics and religion divide many Syrians from one another. But most Syrians would probably agree on at least a few things: they love to talk and laugh, they love to socialize and eat, they love music and dancing, and family is at the center of their lives.

Arranged marriages are still the custom among many Syrians, with mothers primarily in charge of finding suitable young women for their sons. But with today's available technology and access to the Internet and cell phones, this tradition is giving way to young people making their own choices.

Flat bread is often used to scoop up food in place of forks and spoons.

EDUCATION

Syria is justifiably proud of the strides it has made in providing education to all of its citizens. Despite its economic and political woes,

Even as violence gripped the country in 2012, people went about their daily business in many Syrian cities.

the country had a good free basic education system. The estimated literacy rate was 86 percent in 2009.[1] Schooling is required at the primary level, between ages six and 12. The secondary levels consist of a three-year general or vocational training period, followed by either a three-year academic program or another vocational program. The academic program is required for admission into a university. Vocational secondary schools offer studies in industry and agriculture for male students, arts and crafts for female students, and business and computer science for both. Subjects are taught in Arabic, with English and French required as first and second foreign languages in secondary school. Computer literacy is also mandatory at the secondary level.

> In rural Syrian homes, it is common to sit on pillows on the floor rather than on sofas and chairs.

Syria has several private and public universities. Students attending public institutions pay only a small yearly tuition. Major schools include Damascus University, founded in 1923, the country's oldest university, and the University of Aleppo, founded in 1960.

WOMEN IN SYRIA

As in many cultures, traditional Arab culture typically considers women to be inferior to men, and the honor of the family often rests squarely

Syrian students attend an average of 11 years of school.

on the shoulders of daughters and sisters. Despite a constitution that gives Syrian women legal rights equal to those of their male counterparts, the constraints of tradition have prevented many Syrian women from enjoying their rightful place in society.

However, this is slowly changing. Women now take jobs in farms, factories, and office buildings. Though women are poorly represented in government, making up only 12 percent of parliamentarians in 2012, they did fill some high-ranking governmental positions, including the Minister of Tourism, Minister of State for Environment Affairs, and the Minister of Housing and Construction.[2] Women

DRESS AND FASHION

Unlike Muslim-majority countries that follow a strict interpretation of Islamic law, the Syrian Arab Republic has no legal restrictions on women's freedom of dress. The hijab, or headscarf, is worn by women in public with increasing frequency as a personal preference. Head coverings are required when entering mosques, whether during times of prayer or just as a visitor. For the most part, the educated upper classes, especially in cities and particularly the young and career oriented, tend toward Western styles, with women favoring bright colors, jewelry, heavy makeup, and high heels, while men wear slacks and shirts. Kids often wear jeans and T-shirts. In rural and tribal areas, modes of dress are far more traditional. Men wear long kaftans, and women usually wear ankle-length garments that leave only their hands and feet exposed.

A Syrian woman shops for clothing at a Damascus boutique.

have a high profile in higher education, holding many professorships at universities.

Some Syrian women are conflicted by the uprising because they worry what will happen if Assad is toppled from power. While they want his repressive regime to end, they also fear a victory by the Sunni dissidents, whom many believe are backed by the Muslim Brotherhood. In the wake of the ascension to the presidency of Egypt of a Muslim Brotherhood–affiliated candidate, however, these fears may dissipate as Syrians look forward to the prospects of democracy after decades of autocratic rule in which neither men nor women enjoyed basic rights and freedoms.

THE MUSLIM BROTHERHOOD

The Muslim Brotherhood is a political movement founded in Egypt in 1928. The movement combined conservative Islamic beliefs with political aims, and it spread through many countries in the Middle East. Following a 1954 assassination attempt on Egypt's president, the Muslim Brotherhood was banned in Egypt. In 2011, a youth protest movement removed the Egyptian regime, and the Muslim Brotherhood announced that it would return to the Egyptian political scene. Their candidate, Mohammed Morsi, became president in June 2012.

A Syrian rebel runs for cover in February 2012.

SYRIAN REFUGEES AS OF AUGUST 29, 2012

Country	Number of Refugees
Jordan	72,402
Lebanon	57,482
Iraq	18,682
Turkey	80,410
Total	**228,976**[3]

LOOKING AHEAD

By the summer of 2012, Syria had reached an alarming milestone: the country was officially engaged in a civil war. Violent repression continued to escalate, and daily demonstrations took place in many cities and towns.

Newly arrived Syrian refugees rest at
a camp in Jordan.

The sound of gunfire and mortar rounds became routine, and bullet holes
pockmarked buildings. Being arrested for protesting was commonplace,
and many everyday tasks became difficult or even dangerous.

Many Syrians chose to leave their country to escape the violence.
By September 2012, hundreds of thousands had entered Jordan, Lebanon,

Iraq, and Turkey as refugees. In Lebanon's northern regions, more than 1,000 people per week sought refuge.[4] One particular camp in Jordan saw the arrival of approximately 1,400 Syrians each day.[5] Refugees found shelter in camps, schools, and mosques. The United Nations refugee agency worked to improve conditions for fleeing Syrians.

But even amid the conflict, life continued as normal for many Syrians. City streets were clogged with the usual traffic jams, and the people of Damascus went to work and school. On warm evenings after dinner, families strolled down tree-lined streets sharing some baklava. City parks filled with hordes of people talking animatedly in the jasmine-scented air, and old men gathered in coffeehouses to play a Turkish form of backgammon and smoke water pipes. At the same time, the landscape of the Middle East is changing rapidly. The history of religion and politics in Syria is being rewritten in the process.

In early 2012, daily life went on as normal in Syria's peaceful areas.

TIMELINE

5500–4000 BCE	The Tell Zeidan settlement flourishes.
2500 BCE	The city of Ebla, the commercial capital of the region, is thriving.
732 BCE	The Assyrians conquer Syria.
539 BCE	The Babylonians, who had conquered the Assyrians, are themselves defeated by the Persians.
333 BCE	Alexander the Great defeats the Persians and takes over Syria.
269 CE	Queen Zenobia conquers and rules all of Syria.
636	The Umayyads conquer Syria and convert the population to Islam.
ca. 850	The Alawite faith is founded.
1095	The First Crusade is launched, resulting in the slaughter of many Syrians.
1187	The Ayyubids under Saladin defeat the Crusaders and conquer Syria.
1260	The Mongols invade Syria but are stopped by the Mamluks.
1516	Ottomans conquer Syria.

1918	Arab troops, reinforced by British forces, capture Damascus, ending Ottoman rule.
1920	The San Remo Conference legitimizes French rule over Syria.
1940	Syria comes under the jurisdiction of Nazi-occupied France.
1941	French and British forces defeat the Nazi-aligned French forces in Syria.
1946	The last French troops leave Syria.
1947	The Ba'ath Party is founded in Damascus.
1958	Syria and Egypt unite to form the United Arab Republic; Syria secedes in 1961.
1963	The National Council of the Revolutionary Command seizes power.
1971	Hafez al-Assad assumes the presidency after a coup.
2000	President Hafez al-Assad dies of a heart attack; his son Bashar succeeds him.
2011	Antigovernment protests break out in the southern province of Daraa in March.
2012	Protests spread throughout the country, calling for an end to the Assad regime.

FACTS AT YOUR FINGERTIPS

GEOGRAPHY

Official name: Syrian Arab Republic

Area: 71,498 square miles (185,180 sq km)

Climate: Mostly desert or steppe with hot, dry summers; narrow coastal plain with Mediterranean climate

Highest elevation: Mount Hermon, 9,232 feet (2,814 m) above sea level

Lowest elevation: Near Lake Tiberias 656 feet (200 m) below sea level

Significant geographic features: Mediterranean Sea, Syrian Desert

PEOPLE

Population (July 2012 est.): 22,530,746

Most populous city: Aleppo

Ethnic groups: Arabs, Kurds, Armenians, Turks, Circassians

Percent of residents living in urban areas: 56 percent

Life expectancy: 74.92 years (world rank: 93)

Languages: Arabic, Kurdish, Armenian, Aramaic, Circassian, French, English

Religions: Sunni Muslim, 74 percent; other Muslim, 16 percent; Christian, 10 percent; Jewish (very small communities in major cities)

GOVERNMENT AND ECONOMY

Government: republic (de facto one-party rule)

Capital: Damascus

Date of adoption of current constitution: March 13, 1973

Head of state: president

Head of government: prime minister

Legislature: People's Assembly

Currency: Syrian pound

Industries and natural resources: industries: agriculture, petroleum, textiles, food processing; resources: petroleum, phosphates, chrome and manganese ores, cotton, olives, grains and vegetables

NATIONAL SYMBOLS

Holidays: New Year's Day (January 1); Revolution Day (March 8); Independence Day (April 17); Martyrs' Day (May 6); Christmas (December 25)

Flag: Three equal bands of red, white, and black with two green five-pointed stars centered in the middle white band.

National anthem: "Homat el Diyar" (Guardians of the Homeland)

National animal: None; the hawk is the unofficial symbol

KEY PEOPLE

Queen Zenobia, empress of Palmyra, was ruler of Syria in the third century.

Al-Mutanabbi was a renowned tenth-century poet.

Saladin was the founder of Ayyubid dynasty and ruled Syria between 1174 and 1193.

Bashar al-Assad (1965–) became president of Syria after his father's death in 2000.

GOVERNORATES OF SYRIA

Governorate; Capital

Al-Hasakah; Al-Hasakah

Aleppo; Aleppo

Ar-Raqqah; Ar-Raqqah

As-Suwayda; As-Suwayda

Damascus; Damascus

Daraa; Daraa

Dayr al-Zawr; Dayr al-Zawr

Hama; Hama

Homs; Homs

Idlib; Idlib

Latakia; Latakia

Quneitra; Quneitra

Rif Damashq; Damascus

Tartus; Tartus

GLOSSARY

annex

To add new territory to a country or empire.

authoritarian

A form of government emphasizing obedience to authorities rather than personal freedom.

autocratic

Ruled by a person with absolute power.

autonomy

Independence; self-government.

biodiversity

The variety of life in a particular area.

caliph

Historically, a Muslim political and religious leader.

hijab

A head scarf worn by Muslim women.

kaftan

A long, belted tunic.

mosaic

A surface decoration made by inlaying small pieces of variously colored material to form a picture or design.

nomadic

Traveling from place to place rather than settling in a particular area.

secular

Not having a basis in religion.

Semitic

Relating to the language family that includes Hebrew and Arabic or to the people speaking those languages.

socialism

The idea that the means of production should be controlled by the whole society rather than a few people within it.

steppe

An area of flat, treeless grassland.

tell

An artificial mound or hill formed by archeological remains and ruins.

ADDITIONAL RESOURCES

SELECTED BIBLIOGRAPHY

Ball, Warwick. *Syria: A Historical and Architectural Guide*. Northampton, MA: Interlink, 2007. Print.

Darke, Diana. *Syria*. Peterborough, UK: Thomas Cook, 2008. Print.

Hourani, Albert Habib. *A History of the Arab Peoples*. Cambridge, MA: Harvard UP, 2002. Print.

Shoup, John A. *Culture and Customs of Syria*. Westport, CT: Greenwood, 2008. Print.

FURTHER READINGS

Hitti, Philip. *A History of the Arabs*. London: St. Martin's, 2002. Print

Roaf, Michael. *Cultural Atlas of Mesopotamia and the Ancient Near East*. New York: Facts On File, 1990. Print.

WEB LINKS

To learn more about Syria, visit ABDO Publishing Company online at **www.abdopublishing.com**. Web sites about Syria are featured on our Book Links page. These links are routinely monitored and updated to provide the most current information available.

PLACES TO VISIT

If you are ever in Syria, consider checking out these important and interesting sites!

The Great Umayyad Mosque, Damascus

This mosque is cited as the single most remarkable building in Syria and one of the most holy shrines of Islam.

Handicraft Souq, Damascus

This large souq is the best place for souvenir and gift shopping and is conveniently located behind the Damascus National Museum in the heart of Damascus.

Ugarit

The ruins of this ancient city, just north of Latakia on the Mediterranean coast, are where archaeologists found hundreds of clay tablets inscribed with the first phonetic alphabet.

SOURCE NOTES

CHAPTER I. A VISIT TO SYRIA

1. Eric Westervelt. "Al Bara And Serjilla: A Taste of Syria's 'Dead Cities'." *NPR News*. NPR, 22 Oct. 2008. Web. 25 Sept. 2012.

2. Diana Darke. *Syria*. Chalfont Saint Peter, England: Bradt Travel Guides, 2010. Print. 175.

3. Ibid. 179.

CHAPTER 2. GEOGRAPHY: TOPOGRAPHIC DIVERSITY

1. "Euphrates Dam." *Encyclopædia Britannica*. Encyclopædia Britannica, 2012. Web. 25 Sept. 2012.

2. "Euphrates River." *Encyclopædia Britannica*. Encyclopædia Britannica, 2012. Web. 25 Sept. 2012.

3. "Mount Hermon." *Encyclopædia Britannica*. Encyclopædia Britannica, 2012. Web. 25 Sept. 2012.

4. "Barada River." *Encyclopædia Britannica*. Encyclopædia Britannica, 2012. Web. 25 Sept. 2012.

5. Thomas Collelo, ed. "Syria: A Country Study." *Library of Congress*. Library of Congress, 1987. Web. 25 Sept. 2012.

6. "Syria." *Encyclopædia Britannica*. Encyclopædia Britannica, 2012. Web. 25 Sept. 2012.

7. Ibid.

8. Ibid.

9. "Syria." *Weatherbase*. Canty and Associates, 2012. Web. 25 Sept. 2012.

CHAPTER 3. ANIMALS AND NATURE: AN ENVIRONMENT IN PERIL

1. "Species." *Bird Life International*. Bird Life International, 2012. Web. 25 Sept. 2012.

2. "Summary Statistics: Summaries by Country, Table 5, Threatened Species in Each Country." *IUCN Red List of Threatened Species*. International Union for Conservation of Nature and Natural Resources, 2011. Web. 25 Sept. 2012.

3. Samia Madwar. "Defending Diversity." *Syria Today*. Syria Today, Aug. 2010. Web. 25 Sept. 2012.

4. Ibid.

5. "IFAD and Desertification." *International Fund for Agricultural Development.* International Fund for Agricultural Development, n.d. Web. 26 Sept. 2012.

6. Ibid.

CHAPTER 4. HISTORY: OLD LAND, YOUNG COUNTRY

1. "Background Note: Syria." *US State Department.* US State Department, 9 Mar. 2012. Web. 26 Sept. 2012.

2. John M. Riddle. *A History of the Middle Ages, 300–1500.* Lanham, MD: Rowman & Littlefield. Print. 276.

3. Erika Solomon. "Syrian Death Toll Now Tops 30,000: Activist Group." *Reuters.* Reuters, 26 Sept. 2012. Web. 26 Sept. 2012.

CHAPTER 5. PEOPLE: MIDDLE EAST MELTING POT

1. "The World Factbook: Syria." *Central Intelligence Agency.* Central Intelligence Agency, 11 Sept. 2012. Web. 26 Sept. 2012.

2. Ibid.

3. Ibid.

4. "Field Listing: Median Age." *Central Intelligence Agency.* Central Intelligence Agency, 2012. Web. 27 Sept. 2012.

5. "The World Factbook: Syria." *Central Intelligence Agency.* Central Intelligence Agency, 11 Sept. 2012. Web. 27 Sept. 2012.

6. "Syria Overview." *Minority Rights Group International.* Minority Rights Group International, Oct. 2011. Web. 27 Sept. 2012.

7. "Q&A: Armenian Genocide Dispute." *BBC News.* BBC, 5 Mar. 2010. Web. 27 Sept. 2012.

8. Diana Darke. *Syria.* Chalfont Saint Peter, England: Bradt Travel Guides, 2010. Print. 128.

9. Ibid.

10. Adnan Riza Güzel. "Syria's Turkmens, Ethnic Diversity Under Threat." *Today's Zaman.* Today's Zaman, 27 July 2012. Web. 27 Sept. 2012.

11. "The World Factbook: Syria." *Central Intelligence Agency.* Central Intelligence Agency, 11 Sept. 2012. Web. 27 Sept. 2012.

SOURCE NOTES CONTINUED

12. "Slideshow: Who Are The Druze?" *Wide Angle*. PBS, 29 July 2009. Web. 27 Sept. 2012.

13. "Background Note: Syria." *US State Department*. US State Department, 9 Mar. 2012. Web. 27 Sept. 2012.

14. "Syria Overview." *Minority Rights Group International*. Minority Rights Group International, Oct. 2011. Web. 27 Sept. 2012.

CHAPTER 6. CULTURE: ANCIENT INFLUENCES AND MODERN IDEAS

1. John A. Shoup. *Culture and Customs of Syria*. Westport, CT: Greenwood Press, 2008. Print. 65.

CHAPTER 7. POLITICS: A COUNTRY IN UPHEAVAL

1. "Syria." *New York Times*. New York Times, 14 Jun. 2012. Web. 27 Sept. 2012.

2. Joe Sterling. "Daraa: The Spark That Lit the Syrian Flame." *CNN*. CNN, 1 Mar. 2012. Web. 27 Sept. 2012.

3. Khaled Yacoub Oweis. "Syrian Actress Treads New Stage in Syrian Protests." *Reuters*. Reuters, 5 Jan. 2012. Web. 27 Sept. 2012.

4. Ibid.

5. Erika Solomon. "Syrian Death Toll Now Tops 30,000: Activist Group." *Reuters*. Reuters, 26 Sept. 2012. Web. 26 Sept. 2012.

CHAPTER 8. ECONOMICS: CRUDE OIL TO OLIVE OIL

1. Thomas Collelo, ed. "Syria: A Country Study." *Library of Congress*. Library of Congress, 1987. Web. 27 Sept. 2012.

2. Ibid.

3. "The World Factbook: Syria." *Central Intelligence Agency*. Central Intelligence Agency, 11 Sept. 2012. Web. 27 Sept. 2012.

4. Vikas Vij. "Syria Expects Record Olive Oil Production Amid Political Unrest." *Olive Oil Times*. Olive Oil Times, 6 Nov. 2012. Web. 27 Sept. 2012.

5. "Sanctions on Syria Have Cost Country $4 billion, Oil Minister Says." *Fox News.* Associated Press, 23 May 2012. Web. 27 Sept. 2012.

6. "The World Factbook: Syria." *Central Intelligence Agency.* Central Intelligence Agency, 11 Sept. 2012. Web. 27 Sept. 2012.

7. "Syrian Pound, Stock Market Plummet: IMF." *AFP.* AFP, 9 May 2012. Web. 27 Sept. 2012.

8. Ibid.

9. Hadeel al Sayegh. "Syria Prints More Money to Pay Bills." *National.* National, 14 June 2012. Web. 27 Sept. 2012.

CHAPTER 9. SYRIA TODAY

1. "Background Note: Syria." *US State Department.* US State Department, 9 Mar. 2012. Web. 26 Sept. 2012.

2. "Women in National Parliaments." *Inter-Parliamentary Union.* Inter-Parliamentary Union, 31 July 2012. Web. 28 Sept. 2012.

3. "Syria Refugee Outflow Continues, Squeeze on Space in Schools." *AlertNet.* Thomson Reuters Foundation, 31 Aug. 2012. Web. 28 Sept. 2012.

4. Ibid.

5. Ibid.

INDEX

PHOTO CREDITS

Shutterstock Images, cover, 18, 26, 50, 53, 76, 103, 114, 128 (bottom), 130, 131, 133; Elizabeth Shakman Hurd, 2, 11; iStockphoto/Thinkstock, 5 (top and center), 6, 33, 37, 38, 81, 82; iStockphoto, 5 (bottom), 12, 15; Matt Kania/Map Hero, Inc., 8, 21, 28, 62, 110; Styve Reineck/ Shutterstock Images, 22; Pavel Mikoska/Shutterstock Images, 30; Ara Guler/De Agostini/ Getty Images, 40; De Agostini Picture Library/De Agostini/Getty Images, 43, 128 (top); The Bridgeman Art Library/Getty Images, 44; AP Images, 47, 123; Hulton Archives/Getty Images, 54; Bettmann/Corbis/AP Images, 57; Syrian Ministry of Information/AP Images, 59; Rafal Cichawa/ Shutterstock Images, 60; Osama Faisal/AP Images, 64; Bassem Tellawi/AP Images, 68, 75; Dan Balilty/AP Images, 71; Kobby Dagan/Shutterstock Images, 72; Time Life Pictures/Mansell/Time Life Pictures/Getty Images, 79; Alexandre Meneghini/AP Images, 85; Muzaffar Salman/AP Images, 87, 119; Rodrigo Abd/AP Images, 89; David Goldman/AP Images, 90; Paul Cowan/Shutterstock Images, 92, 132; Hussein Malla/AP Images, 95, 100, 129 (top); Hassan Ammar/AP Images, 99, 129 (bottom); Dudarev Mikhail/Shutterstock Images, 104; Kathy Willens/AP Images, 107; Harry Koundakjian/AP Images, 113; Kaveh Kazemi/Getty Images, 116; Ola Rifai/AP Images, 120; Mohammad Hannon/AP Images, 125; Rodrigo Abd/AP Images, 126